THE
DUFFER'S
GUIDE TO
BOOZE

Gren.

COLUMBUS BOOKS
LONDON

Other books in the Duffer's series:
The Official Duffer's Rules of Golf (John Noble)
The Official Duffer's Rules of Tennis (Bob Adams)
The Duffer's Guide to Golf: A Second Slice (Gren)
The Duffer's Guide to Rugby (Gren)
The Duffer's Guide to Greece (Gren)
The Duffer's Guide to Spain (Gren)
The Duffer's Guide to Coarse Fishing (Mike Gordon)
The Duffer's Guide to Cricket (Gren)

The Duffer's Guide to Snooker (Mike Gordon)
The Duffer's Guide to Rugby: Yet Another Try (Gren)

Copyright © 1985 Gren of the *South Wales Echo*

First published in Great Britain in 1985 by
Columbus Books
Devonshire House, 29 Elmfield Road, Bromley, Kent BR1 1LT

Printed and bound by Clark Constable,
Edinburgh, London, Melbourne

ISBN 0 86287 233 2

CONTENTS

Introduction: 5

Types of Booze: 6
    The lighter drinks
    The silly drinks
    The AND drinks
    The serious drinks

Drinking Types: 11
    The bar bore
    The Major
    The young executive
    The lonely housewife
    The expense-account boozer
    The CamRA type
    'You're wasting your time. . .'
    The beer-swiller

The Lady Drinker: 20
    'Medium dry sherry. . .'
    'Bacardi and coke'
    'Manhattan, darling'
    'Half a bitter. . .'
    'Gimme a treble whisky. . .'
    'Port and lemon. . .'

Hangover Cures: 27
    Two pints of water
    The combination drink
    Stay in bed
    The cold shower

Types of Public House: 32
    The estate pub
    The town pub
    The village inn
    The country pub
    The swinging spot

I Drink Because. . .: 38

How to Tell When You Are Drunk: 48
    Slurred speech
    Double vision
    Staggering
    Unable to remember. . .
    Becoming stroppy
    The raving beauty syndrome

Places to Drink: 55
    Pubs
    Clubs
    Hotel bars
    Sleazy clubs
    At home
    Park bench

Helpful Hints: 62
    Last orders
    Offer to buy a drink. . .
    The ice ploy
    Carrying drinks
    Never apologize. . .
    Flirting
    Returning a pint
    Being complimentary
    The crowded bar

Boozer's Jargon: 72

Bar Staff: 76
    The landlord
    The blowzy blonde barmaid
    The dolly bird barmaid
    The barman bouncer

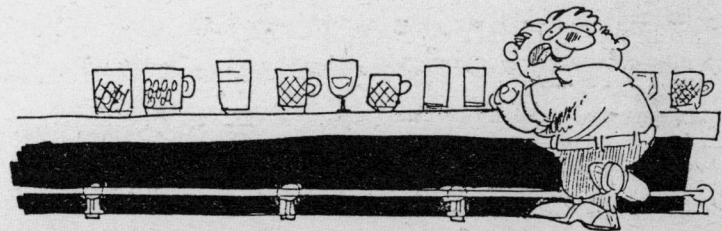

Introduction

Ever since that fateful day in the Garden of Eden when Adam said to Eve, "'Ello, darlin', what's yours?", boozing has developed to become an art form.

We therefore offer this guide to the boozing duffer to help him or her stagger through the complicated social network that is held together by alcoholic occasions.

Come with us, duffer boozer. Never again will you put a cherry or a slice of lemon in your half pint of bitter — or demurely request a medium dry sherry shandy.

Types of Booze

There are basically four groups of alcoholic drink, and one should beware leaping about between them swigging anything on offer, unless, of course, one is researching the hangover.

The lighter drinks

These are, of course, the shandies, the almost non-alcoholic lagers and the 'make-mine-a-small-gin-in-a-pint-pot-and-top-it-up-with-orange-squash' type of drink.

The beauty of this type of drink is that it is, from a drunken point of view, very safe to drink. Your bloated body will refuse to take any more liquid well before the alcohol has had chance to fuddle your brain, which serves you right for drinking such muck.

It also has the drawback that, as you're the only sober person left at the bar, you're also the only one who remembers it's your round.

Duffers should beware the lighter drinks.

The silly drinks

The serious duffer will avoid silly drinks. They were invented for giggly girls and pseudo-trendy twits. Silly drinks are to real drinks what Dean Martin is to the temperance movement.

Silly drinks are mainly fad drinks or cocktails with silly names like Harvey Wallbanger, Buck's Fizz, Tequilla Sunrise and Benidorm Surprise.

The boozing duffer can almost always tell when he has been sipping a silly drink, usually because there's a little paper umbrella or plastic swizzle stick stuck up his nostrils.

The AND drinks

The AND drinks are spirits to which a splash (or more) of something has been added, or a decent strong British beer (not the foreign muck) is accompanied by some essential comestible – hence their being called 'and' drinks. Gin AND tonic, scotch AND dry, pint AND a packet of crisps, etc. etc.

The serious drinks

The duffer should never ever accept a glass of serious drink. These are the no-nonsense drinks that are knocked back by hard professional drinkers (and cowboy 'baddies' in western films).

Serious drinks are neat whisky, brandy, gin, or vodka-type drinks, never singles – and all in the same glass, too, for some of the better professional drinkers.

A truly-serious-drinks drinker will be horrified if you add ice to his scotch or suggest he may require a tonic with his vodka.

Drinking Types

Drinkers fall into easily recognizable types as they sip, swig or shake their drinking hours away.

A lonely duffer boozer will quickly be accepted in to the company of fellow boozers by offering the time-honoured ritual greeting of 'Wotjeravinen?'. No matter what their type, the duffer will immediately be surrounded by new friends.

The bar bore

The bar bore gets everwhere. In the golf club he's the one describing in great detail every shot played in his last eighteen holes. In the sleazy club he's the one who's cornered you with drunken conversation while you're trying to watch the stripper. In the pub he's the chap who waylays you with a series of terrible jokes that you've heard before, many times.

Duffers who find themselves stuck with the bar bore should try the old pub game of 'out-bore the bore', which can be fun if, of course, you can get a word in to start the game.

The Major

The Major can be seen in every country pub. He bristles, tweeds and booms his opinions to all. His barked requests for a double scotch strike terror into any new barmaid.

His main topic of conversation always revolves around great drinking feats in the mess at Berlin or Kuala Lumpur, the memories of which cause his eyes to water merrily and his sweaty red nose to throb.

The young executive

The young executive type is never seen alone. He and his young executive friends are always in the best bar of whatever establishment they decide to honour with their presence.

They are equally anxious to impress others as they loudly talk of their company's fringe benefits, marketing policies or recession-fighting plans.

Young executives often seem to request strange drinks: 'I'll have Pernod with soda and it's Campari and Tizer with a slice of lemon for Roger and a glass of Algerian red with a drop of cider for Julian.'

The lonely housewife

The lonely housewife is a difficult type for the boozing duffer to spot because she drinks mainly at home, sipping her medium dry sherry until early evening, whereupon she greets her man with his reviving scotch while getting stuck into the vodka herself.

When she does venture out, she may be seen at the local supermarket skulking at the checkout — her latest nest of bottles hidden from view by boxes of All-Bran and boil-in-the-bag meals.

Duffers will find it's rewarding always to have a kind word for the lonely housewife and, if possible, to buy her a drink.

The expense-account boozer

This drinker likes to play the big spender, sending bottles of the best wine to an acquaintance he's spotted in the far corner of the bar's restaurant or insisting you have a treble scotch when you hate the stuff and have in any case been drinking port all night.

Duffers should avoid drinking with expense-account types as it's almost impossible to leave them while your legs still work properly.

The CamRA type

CamRA, as the duffer will soon find, stands for the CAMpaign for Real Ale. Its members should be avoided at all costs. No sooner has the boozing duffer begun to enjoy a particular beer when the CamRA type will tell you exactly why he's not really enjoying it at all.

The CamRA type will rhapsodize with his little CamRA friends about a pint of Old Belch he once had at a backwoods pub he stumbled across while lost in a fog on Exmoor, and then openly deride the latest bitter put on at the pub next door – which the duffer will be afraid to admit he rather enjoys.

It's good fun to annoy CamRA people – you can do this by asking for a lager shandy when they're paying.

17

The 'you're-wasting-your-time-if-you're-trying-to-get-me-drunk' type

This lady is a very experienced drinker and the duffer boozer would do well to study her technique. She can drink anyone under the table while she remains sober and thirsty, even after the bar has run dry.

She has spent a lifetime seeing off would-be Romeos whose alcohol-assisted efforts have backfired.

The beer-swiller

The beer-swiller can be seen in every bar. Even in the twee cocktail bar the swiller will demand his pint of bitter and will not be put off receiving it by precious excuses from a delicate barman.

He'll drink only beer and thinks that anyone who drinks anything else is a fairy, even men who drink half-pints. Even standing next to a half-pint drinker in the toilets is more than he can tolerate.

The Lady Drinker

The experienced boozer can tell, just by looking at her, what a lady will drink. There should never be any need to ask her – armed with this trusty guide, you can take one good look at her and order her a drink.

However, as a boozing duffer you should, at this stage of your boozing career, always ask, otherwise you may end up drinking a mis-ordered Tequilla Sunrise or Benidorm Surprise – yuck!

'A medium dry sherry for me, please'

This lady is usually very cheap to take for a drink. Sipping her medium dry sherry for hours on end, she continually fidgets with her pearls while her other hand locks her handbag in a vice-like grip.

She will never let drink get the better of her. It seems the alcohol escapes in a terrified evaporation as the glass is raised to her thin-lipped mouth.

'A Bacardi and coke, please'

This lady hasn't ever forgotten her wonderful holiday in Majorca when she discovered Bacardi and coke and drank the stuff every night for two wonderful weeks. She now tries to relive that magical experience, failing to do so because her pub serves up singles, which really do not match up to that Spanish Romeo barman's sloshed-up triples, which she still remembers with nostalgia.

'A Manhattan-with-all-the-trimmings, darling'

This type of lady drinker always comes in a pair – the other being her Hooray Henry escort.

She'll sip away at the latest fashionable cocktail as she sits perched on a bar stool smoking strange, smelly cigarettes from a long holder.

The duffer will find great satisfaction in stunning into horrified silence the lady who, after ordering something with a cherry in it, hears *him* ordering a pint with a spud in it.

'Half a bitter in a handle glass'

She's usually come directly off some picket line or from acting as secretary to some way-out arts group.

She caresses her glass as she gives forth about equal rights for left-handed Welsh one-eyed Jews or how she and one or two others are going to bring the country to its knees by boycotting imported Taiwanese corn dollies.

Male duffer boozers should seek out this type of lady — she always pays her round.

24

'Gimme a treble whisky, easy on the ice'

This is usually the career woman who manages to cope with a very demanding job while bringing up three genius children, running a marvellously well-organized home – and of course she's also very involved in a local charity organization when it doesn't clash with her professional committee work, for which she's the chairperson.

The duffer must be very quick to spot this type. She tends not to stand still long.

'Port 'n' lemon for me, luv'

She sits happily in any corner of any pub, chatting to kings or peasants alike, puffing away on her ciggy. On Saturday evenings, after about eight tots of her favourite tipple, her eyes mist up and she quietly sings Vera Lynn songs to anyone who will listen.

The port-and-lemon type is the life and soul of any local. But duffers beware – this sweet lady will drink you under the table.

Hangover cures

There are many hangover cures. Every drinker you meet will readily reveal one that he guarantees to work.

If you, the duffer boozer, should suffer a hangover, do the decent thing – lie back and enjoy it as you mutter, like millions before you, the immortal words, 'Never again'.

Drink two pints of water before you go to bed

This one almost works because if you drink your two pints of cold water after an evening of throwing a steady stream of alcohol down your throat, it stands to reason that you'll be up very many times during the night to visit the bathroom. This is where the cure becomes *effective* — all that walking back and forth to the loo sobers you up and your hangover will begin to fade.

The combination drink

There are many sworn remedies based on combinations of drinks – such as tomato juice and worcester sauce, egg and vinegar, brandy and port, yoghurt and fresh orange juice, and so on.

The rationale for these cures is that they make you feel so awful that the original hangover pales into insignificance.

Stay in bed

This is the best of all hangover remedies – it doesn't cure your hangover but it makes it as bearable as possible.

To know if your hangover has passed, get a friend to ask if you'd like a glass of your favourite tipple. If you do, you're cured. So get up.

The cold shower

This is a very painful remedy. Your naked, almost lifeless body is slouched under a freezing cold shower. For any rejuvenation at all to take place, you must endure the numbing pain for at least thirty minutes.

The cold-shower treatment does work, but you must ask yourself whether you wouldn't prefer the hangover you've got to the pneumonia you're going to get.

31

Types of Public House

There are as many kinds of pub as there are veins on a landlord's nose. You, the duffer, fresh and new to the boozing world, have a wonderful opportunity before you to try every type of pub many times, seeking out your favourite — until you realize that there is no such thing as a bad pub.

The estate pub

This is the pub purpose-built on a housing estate
in the hope of catching all the local business.

It's very functional and a great place to meet
your neighbours for a good gossip. The residents'
association always meets in this type of pub.

The town pub

This pub is schizophrenic — during the lunch period it's a happy, chirpy, friendly place where young office workers enjoy the odd gassy half and a ploughman's while the senior executives discuss business deals over a lasagne and salad washed down with gins and tonics.

The evenings, however, usually sees the same pub quietly hosting lonely drinkers as the bar staff, worn out and hung over from the lunchtime activity, eagerly await the moment for Stop Tap.

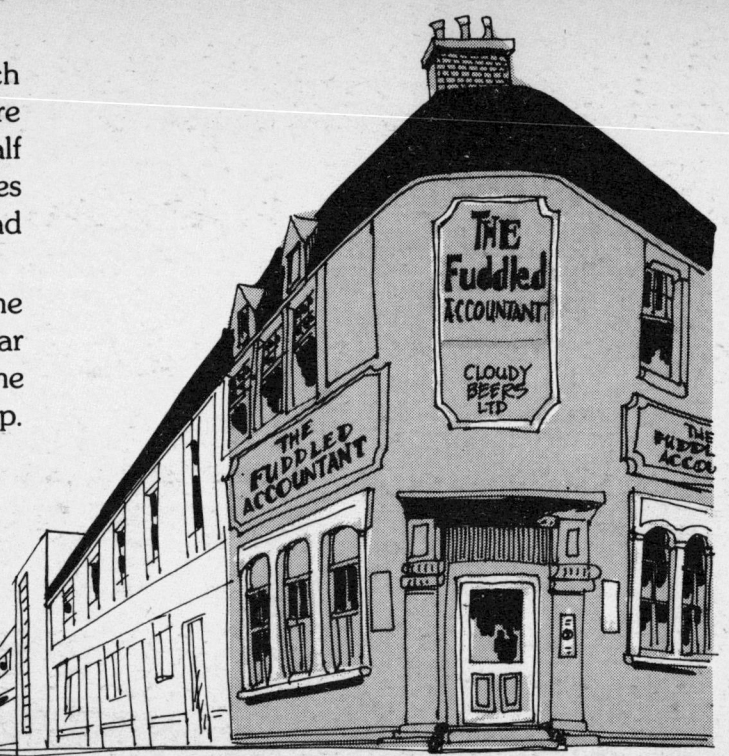

The village inn

This is usually a dowdy, very unpretentious couple of converted terrace houses in which there are hardly any customer comforts — or customer anything.

The place is so unattractive that beer snobs love it — managing to convince themselves that the landlord 'keeps a good barrel'.

Duffers, being uninitiated in the ways of the beer snob, cannot usually appreciate the finer points of this type of watering-hole. Nor can most others.

The country pub

This lovely, twee pub tries to suggest the atmosphere of the coaching inns of yesteryear – while the prices are of next year.

In the summer what could be better than relaxing in its garden playing traditional country games, such as guessing how many gnats will drown in your pint before you drink it?

And in the winter what better way to relax could there be than sitting in front of the huge log fire dodging the missile sparks that hurtle towards you?

Country pub food is usually great, too.

The swinging spot

One of the great problems in the Swinging Spot pub is that you have great difficulty in finding the bar. It's there somewhere in the gloom, hidden away behind music machines, huge video screens, flashing lights and speakers.

When you eventually find it, it's tended by a young, scrawny girl who doesn't know her lager from her mild, serves you double scotch in a Pernod glass and puts your change on the bar in a pool of beer.

Duffers should never drink in a Swinging Spot pub. It could put you off boozing for life.

37

I drink because. . .

All boozers owe it to themselves to analyze why
they are drinking. Nothing is more guaranteed to
put anyone off their drink than the thought that
it's being done without a good reason.

For you, the boozing duffer, to get the most out
of being merrily half-stoned you should select
one of the following reasons, whichever takes
your fancy.

I'm tense.

I'm celebrating.

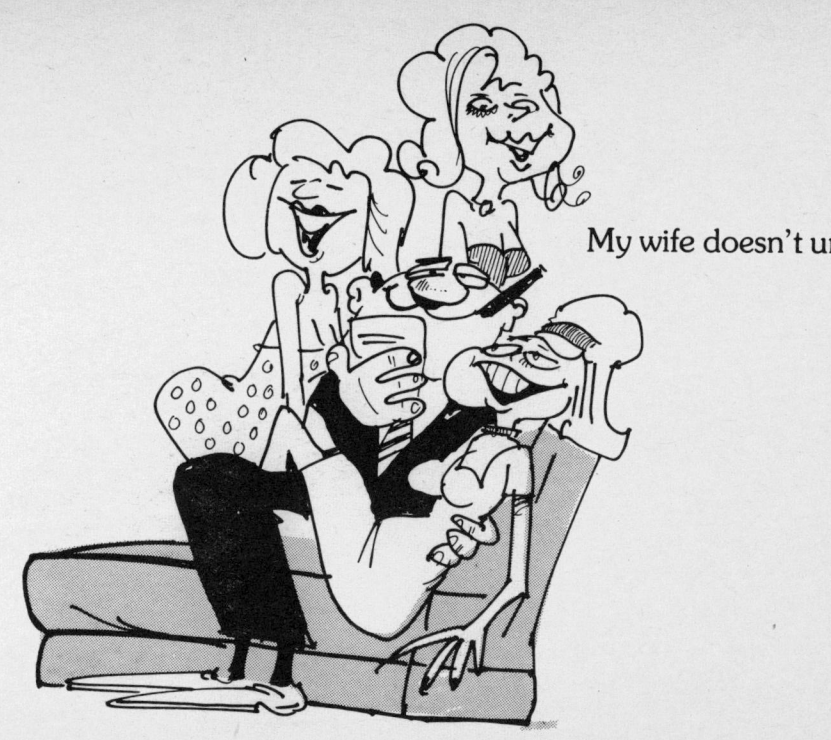

My wife doesn't understand me.

My wife *does* understand me.

I'm always thirsty.

43

I need a pick-me-up.

I need Dutch courage.

To forget.

I just enjoy being drunk.

How to tell when you are drunk

One of the great problems with boozing is that the more one has to drink the more one is likely to be unaware that one is drunk.

This is obviously dangerous – but even more so for the duffer, who has to wait for some well-meaning friend to tell him he's drunk because as a newcomer to the game he doesn't notice the signs that would immediately indicate to an experienced boozer that he's had enough.

Duffers should always be on the alert to spot the following symptoms.

Slurred speech

This very embarrassing situation comes about when your brain has told your tongue to say something quite simple like 'Hello, Samantha, how are you?' but your tongue says 'Ehllo-Samantherowyooo?'. You ask your tongue to try again and this time, after you've concentrated hard, it says 'Losmanfahowryoooo'.

You then decide to overcome the embarrassment of your tongue not working by the use of your winning smile, which also doesn't behave — coming over as a leering, dribbling grin.

You therefore decide to throw yourself upon her mercy and apologize with a straightforward 'I'm sorry', which comes out as 'Mmmshorry' — and, in saying it, you slop your pint of Old Wart Special all over her new outfit.

Double vision

This should immediately indicate to you that your body has received far too much alcohol. You can't focus properly and the person you are over-confidently talking to has become twins.

You try to correct this by closing one eye and peering steadfastly. This is taken by those around you to mean that you're having some sort of fit — so go back to keeping both eyes open and suffering double vision: it causes less panic.

Staggering

If when walking towards the bar for the umpteenth time with your glass firmly clenched in your fist your legs take you in a direction which you have not intended, you are probably drunk (a condition which is known in the medical profession as *Stonedus anewtus*).

As you stagger towards your goal colliding with fellow-drinkers, bumping into furniture, falling over the pub dog, you can be sure that your body is suggesting you have had enough. As you're having such difficulty in getting to the bar you probably *will* stop drinking anyway — but the decision will have been taken by your legs, not your brain.

51

Unable to remember who you are

You can be sure you should stop drinking if when you look in the mirror of the washroom you vaguely recognize the reflection as being a person you know but can't think where you've met him before (and can't remember his name either).

This might frighten you into joining groups of fellow-drinkers in the hope that one will introduce you to another, hence jogging your stupefied memory.

This cure is, of course, to stop drinking and lie down somewhere. Within five or six hours you will remember the forgotten name — with due shame and embarrassment.

Becoming stroppy

This is just one of many alterations to your normal behaviour pattern which should indicate that you, the duffer, have exceeded your alcohol capacity. Some other indications include holding forth on subjects you know nothing about and thinking you have hidden talents for debate.

These, of course, are forerunners to 'becoming stroppy', which usually entails pointing out to bar staff their personal shortcomings or making a point with the aid of your prodding finger.

Duffers can usually tell when they have become stroppy. Someone kindly points it out to them by smacking them playfully on the nose.

The raving beauty syndrome

This is a particularly vicious side-effect of having had too much too drink and can, for an unsuspecting duffer, have very nasty consequences.

It often seems that the lady who, when you were stone-cold sober, struck you as being a very ordinary-looking type, and certainly nothing special, all of a sudden after a few drinks looks to you like a raving beauty. This is a sure sign of being drunk.

Stop drinking immediately before you make rash promises or even rasher proposals.

HASH ANYONE EVER TOLD YOU, MISH, THAT YOU BEAR A SHTRIKING RESHEMBLANCE TO JOAN COLLINSH?

Places to drink

Duffer boozers will soon discover their favourite places to drink. The choice is wide, and gradually, by trial and error, they will discover the joys of supping in certain types of watering-hole.

Pubs

Probably the most popular of all drinking establishments are the public houses, where strangers can soon find themselves in jolly company as soon as they offer to buy a round.

Boozing duffers should always go to pubs.

Clubs

Clubs can be fun but invariably they are set up within a sporting or political framework. So the duffer drinker who hates golf could find himself bored stiff by the golf chat or politically at odds with fellow boozers. While he may be able to cope with the company for the first few drinks, it will become increasingly difficult for him to swallow his political or sporting opinions, and punch-ups may tend to occur.

Duffers shouldn't join such clubs.

Hotel bars

The duffer boozer should only be seen drinking in an hotel bar if he is having a drink before dining at the hotel, meeting someone who is staying there, or looking for some after-hours boozing by protesting, as he's being ejected from the bar, that he's an hotel guest.

Another good reason for a duffer not to drink in hotel bars is that they are usually expensive — but, on the other hand, usually have free peanuts and crisps on the bar counter.

Sleazy clubs

As a boozing duffer must never, ever, drink at a sleazy club. You'll be charged at least three times the usual price for a pint of weak, warm beer and four times over the norm for spirits, this on top of paying a ridiculous cover charge for the dubious privilege of seeing a tatty, ageing stripper go through a series of gyrations that are guaranteed to make your beer go even flatter.

At home

There are several advantages to drinking at home. It's comfortable, you don't have to wait to be served — and there are no irritating licensing hours.

There are, of course, drawbacks — your wife won't let you throw crisp packets or fag-ends on to the floor and most of all you'll miss chatting up the barmaids.

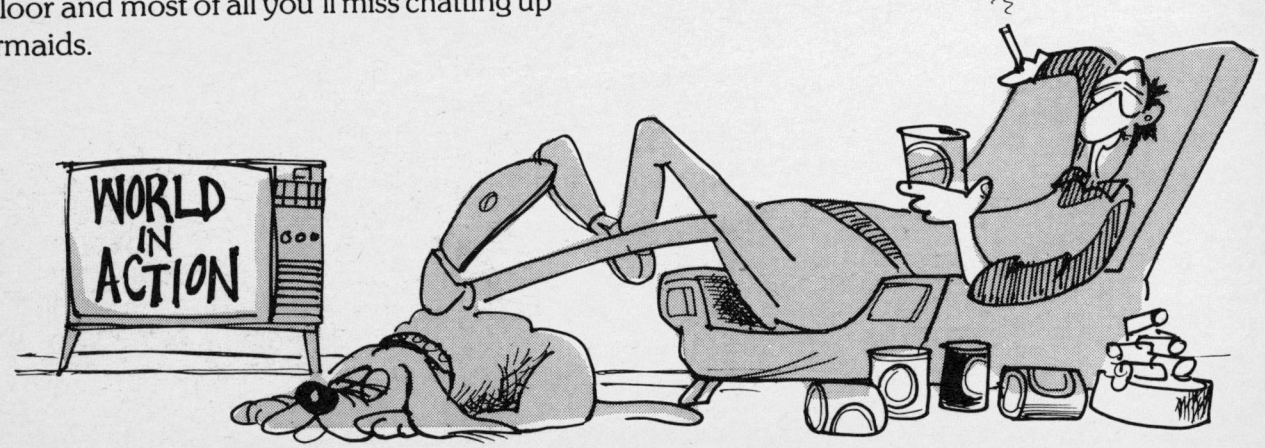

Park bench

The duffer should never drink on a park bench. It attracts the wrong sort of friends and people who used to seek out your company will somehow pretend not to have noticed you.

Helpful Hints

Like every other profession, boozing has its tricks of the trade, which, if properly employed, will either overcome the problems of supping or make the hours spent doing so even more pleasurable.

When the landlord shouts, 'Last orders, please', never say, 'I bequeath my liver to medical science'. He's heard it before and it annoys him.

Offer to buy someone a drink only when:

(1) they're in the middle of ordering a large, complicated round (they'll decline your offer and buy you one instead);

(2) after you know it's 'stop tap'.

Always put double the amount of ice in your wife's drink that you put in yours. This way she'll be flattered by your generosity, thinking you're buying her doubles.

Never ever carry drinks by putting your grubby fingers inside the glasses.

The alcohol will burn any cuts or grazes you may have on them.

Never bother to apologize for bumping into any-one, making them slop their drinks as you push your way to the bar.

Wait until you again collide with them as you return from the bar, then apologize for both occasions.

Never flirt with the blonde behind the bar – she may be the landlord's wife.

Never ever return a pint complaining that it's undrinkable until you have drunk more than half of it. Then demand a fresh one.

Always compliment your lady friend on how the new colour of her once-white dress suits her after you've slopped red wine over it.

When standing at the back of a very crowded bar, your journey to the front will be speedier if you say in a loud voice, 'Do you think I should be drinking while I've got mumps?'

Boozers' Jargon

Like the medics and lawyers, boozers like to disguise their art by surrounding it with the mystique of complicated language.

Open tap   The bar is open for serving

I'm in the chair...
  My shout!
  My round! } I'm buying the drinks
  I'm asking
My honour...

Stop tap   The bar has stopped serving

Short A barman who is under five feet tall

Single One measure of the optic,
which you order for someone
else on your round

Double Twice the normal optic
measure, which you ask for on
someone else's round

Dry A slightly bitter drink which you get when you should have ordered a medium

Sweet Something you get when you want dry or medium

Medium A fairly sweet drink which you get when you want dry

ARE YOU THE MEDIUM?

I THINK THAT'S THE SWEET.

74

Foreign muck Any imported beer or lager

One for the road The one you have that ensures that you'll have to stop and get out of the car on the way home

Merry
Drunk
Smashed
Pole-axed
Stoned
Intoxicated
Legless
Polluted
Half-cut
Bashed
Paralytic
Zonked
Tired and emotional
Brahms and Liszt
Plastered
Comatose
P——d
Blotto
Pie-eyed
Squiffy
Tiddly

Inebriated

Bar Staff

People who work on the 'other side' of the bar are employed in that capacity because they are warm, friendly, outgoing types who enjoy meeting people, can happily chat on most subjects and, above all, make you feel very welcome. Well, that's the theory, anyway.

Instead, duffers are likely to be greeted by one of the following types.

The landlord

'Mine host' knows all the regulars by name and pretends he knows exactly what they want when they ask for 'the usual, please'.

The landlord seems to be able to drink all day without getting drunk, but gets furious if he catches anyone watering his beer or spirits because he's probably done it himself already.

The blowzy blonde barmaid

Calling everyone 'love' and dispensing warm, earthy humour while she cheerfully serves you, she'll also lend a sympathetic ear to your problems.

The blowzy blonde is often related to the landlord – but only by marriage.

78

The dollybird barmaid

She's usually employed just as decoration, to attract the customers or to distract their minds from a nagging suspicion that the drinks have been watered.

She can't pour a decent pint or calculate correct change and can be relied upon to serve up your gin and tonic without ice and lemon.

Men will never complain, happily accepting her shortcomings in return for the illusion that her flirtatious conversation could lead to a close acquaintance.

The barman/bouncer

This man is employed in a dual capacity. If there's no one to thump or throw out of the place, he has to serve behind the bar, but he doesn't enjoy this as much as thumping customers.

This type is usually found in a sleazy bar. Duffers who have heeded our earlier advice not to frequent such establishments are unlikely to encounter this particular species.

80